KONVERSATIONS
— IN THE —
DARK

KONVERSATIONS
IN THE
DARK

VANESSA G. CHEEK

authorHOUSE®

AuthorHouse™ LLC
1663 Liberty Drive
Bloomington, IN 47403
www.authorhouse.com
Phone: 1-800-839-8640

Published by AuthorHouse   12/16/2013

ISBN: 978-1-4918-4469-4 (sc)
ISBN: 978-1-4918-4468-7 (e)

Library of Congress Control Number: 2013923066

December 01, 2009

Dear Readers,

This book came about because I was sick and tired of reading books about young men and women living in a world of drugs and crime. I know that they are still prevalent but that is not everyone's lifestyle. I have many friends who are living with the virus that causes AIDS. They are not into drugs or a life of crime. We are simply people who are not going to let life beat us up or tear us down. We are here to stay and we are going to live life like never before.

My friends came together with me to share their stories and the true meaning of life and living with HIV/AIDS. When we could have thrown in the towel, we did not. All stories are based on both fact and fiction. The name of this book is called "Konversations In The Dark" because HIV and AIDS is a subject no one wants to talk about. I hope you enjoy this book as much as I've enjoyed writing it. I want each person to realize this could easily be your story, so please use protection at all times.

As I wrote each story, I found myself in each of these women in one way or another. I really want everyone that reads this book to be honest and true to themselves because it could've been you too. I would like to thank everyone who decided to share their story. Please know that I am very proud of you and that your story will make a difference.

Sincerely,

Vanessa C.

P.S. God has not given me the spirit of fear, but of love, power, and a sound mind. (II Timothy 1:7 King James)

SIMONE

I've watched so many family members die from the virus that causes AIDS. Even those experiences didn't ease my despair when I was diagnosed as being HIV positive in 1995. I felt like I was in a head on collision with a tractor trailer, spinning around in circles as I watched flashes of colors coming towards me. I heard a voice faintly saying, "Miss, Miss" as I turned my head, I realized I was still sitting in my doctor's office. I gave her a look and got up from the chair. I can't remember how I got home but I do recall being awakened by someone screaming and it sounded as though the person was in agony. I kept saying to myself "Oh my God I wish they would stop all that screaming and what on earth could have happened that they were in so much pain." As I sat up in bed, took a glance in the mirror and realized I was the lunatic doing the loud screaming.

One of my neighbors called my sister and she arrived in what seemed like seconds. I can remember her holding me very tight and she was praying for me too. I was immediately hospitalized for mental exhaustion. While in the hospital I had a therapist who told me I did not have to be afraid of being HIV positive and that people are living longer because there are medications, and support groups. Each day when I met with my therapist, it seemed like she had new and exciting things to tell me about HIV. She even got me started with a support group at the hospital.

Now that I am out of the hospital I've joined a church and a couple of support groups. I have new friends and we do not just sit and talk about HIV or medication we talk about life and how to live it more abundantly. I'm living with HIV and if it wants to live with me it better be under subjection and the only way it can do that is by me taking my medication and keeping my doctor's appointments. It has been a long journey. I have learned so much and I've met so many people that have helped me to be where I am and who I am. So when someone asked "How did I get the virus, or who gave it to me?" I respond by asking them does it really matter because it's not that important to me anymore. What is important to me is that I am living with no hang ups and no hidden anger. God has blessed me to the utmost.

Sincerely,

Simone
Life is just beginning.

CORA

I am Cora and I've heard rumors that the man I was living with was sleeping with a female who was positive and sick. Therefore, during my yearly physical for my job I asked them to test me for HIV. When I got my results back it was a double whammy. Never in a million years did I think that I would be living with a man who has the virus that causes AIDS nor did I think he would cheat on me. Now I had proof because my HIV test result was positive which let me know the rumor was true and he cheated with a woman that was positive. I told him my status and told him to get tested. He was tested and they immediately had him take medication. We tried to make it work but I had to let him go when he refused to wear condoms. I told my good friend Gwen about my status and she gave me the love and support that I needed.

A few years later in 2005 after reviewing my T-cell count result my doctor suggested that I start taking medication. I've never had a reaction from any medication. Although I've heard a lot of horror stories about various side effects of medications, my doctor informed me that everybody is different and what someone else's body might go through doesn't mean my body will so I decided that it was better for me to take the medication than nothing at all.

I told my baby daughter first and she took it very well. I will always remember what she said and I quote "It is what it is and no matter what we will deal with it" and that is just what we are doing just dealing with it.

I got involved with the women's wellness group because I wanted to meet women living with the virus and share what we are going through on a daily basis. I've learned to give so much of myself that I cannot see myself being anywhere else but in a support group. I'm not in a relationship at this time because I have learned that I have trust issues and by having this virus, I would be horrified if I gave this virus to someone. Having this virus taught me that I am responsible for my own body and now I have regular check-ups. When I feel that something is going on with my body that I do not understand I call my doctor.

The reason I am telling my story is so that those who do not have the virus continue to protect themselves so they won't get it. The people who do have HIV must realize that we are our brother's keeper and take responsibility for your own action.

Much love,

Cora
There is no failure in God.

MY UNCLE

My uncle was a petite gentleman with an enormous yet beautiful personality. His skin was a warm caramel brown, his eyes were like brown marbles with a sparkle and he had coffee cooler lips and a distinguished laugh that if you heard it you knew it was him. His hair was short and nappy with each strand of hair having its very own curl and you had to really comb it and grease it to keep it laid down. My uncle was a tailor who took pride in his work, he loved people, and he loved good conversations too.

My uncle never married. His sexuality was questionable for some people. I've never seen him with a man or a woman and I didn't care. He was my uncle and he was very good to me. He made me feel important and he loved me for me. I never felt that I had to put a label on him or anyone else as far as that matters.

He became a member of my mother's church and gave his life to Jesus Christ. The church family fell in love with him and he loved the church. You can tell he finally felt like he belonged and he wanted to be involved in the church. My uncle was HIV positive. The stigma that comes with HIV and AIDS made my uncle decide that it would be best that we would not mention it to any family member. We honored his request. During his last days he always made you feel like you were special and he would give you a special wink in a room full of people, which was his way of letting you know that he noticed and loved you.

AIDS destroyed his body. I saw him crawl when he could no longer walk. He slept on the floor when the bed was uncomfortable for his fragile body. I heard him cry out to God when the pain was too much for him to bear and most of all I saw him give up the ghost when God told him to come on home. The room became calm and peaceful; a cool breeze filled the room and in a wink of an eye he was in glory.

Little did I know a few years after his death, I would be diagnosed with the virus that causes AIDS.

Sincerely,

Simone
I've shared my uncle's story, now what will my story be?

KAREN

I was married for twenty-five years to my high school sweetheart. We have three children; two boys and one girl. I was a stay at home wife and mother and since my husband wanted it that way, that's what I did. To make my days go by faster I decided to take cooking classes, pottery, sewing, so if there was a class I took it and I also joined the PTA and coached soccer. I really just wanted to be there for my husband and children. When my husband wanted to have sports night for his friends at our home, I was so proud because that meant I could show off the cooking skills I've learned from all the different cooking classes I had taken.

On May 18, 2004, my husband Roger caught a terrible cold. He did not want to go to the hospital and when I realized that I could not nurse him back to health, I called my son. Since he was nurse, he came over with his instruments and told me that it did not look good and we should take him to the emergency room immediately. My husband had PCP Pneumonia. I had no idea what that meant but by the look on my son's face, I knew it was serious so I asked my son, "What did that mean?" He said, "mom let's wait to see the blood work results." When the blood work came back, the nurse told me that my husband, the man I had loved all my life had AIDS. I was mad as hell. I just stared into his eyes for what seemed like an eternity and then I said, "Tell me how and do not lie to me." After twenty-five years of marriage, my relationship was over. Not only did Roger have AIDS he was also homosexual. I left the hospital, went home got in bed and cried for weeks. Finally, my daughter came over telling me to get it together because my life was not over and I needed to be tested.

I was tested and I am not positive thank you Jesus. Roger and I got divorced. I went to technical school for nursing. I also joined a gym. Roger is doing well. I want the best for him. My friends looked at me with disbelief when I told them I had no idea he was gay. I may have been too close to see it or maybe I simply over looked it but I would not change my life story even if I could. Roger and I had great life. I love him and I always will. When people read my story, I want them to know that this can happen to anyone but you might not be as blessed as I have been. I don't know why some women get the virus and others don't. I say protect yourselves because you never know.

Sincerely,

Karen
The wife

SASHA

After my divorce in 2001, my self-esteem was down in the basement, which left me looking for love in all the wrong places. I was dating recklessly having unprotected sex. I was in relationships with men, who did not even know how to spell commitment or know the definition of it. Let's face it; no one should be in a relationship without a commitment. One day I just woke up sitting on my couch and I did an inventory of my life and realized I needed to love myself.

In March 2008, I started feeling ill with flu like systems so I made an appointment with my doctor. Then later in the same year, I had problems breathing so I went into the emergency room. A nurse asked had I ever taken a HIV test and I said yes two years ago and it came back negative. She asked me would I mind taking another and I said sure why not, then that test came back positive.

My doctor put me in the Intensive Care Unit and for weeks my family came to my rescue once they heard I was in ICU. My doctors felt that they needed to put me in an induced coma. My momma came up from the south and like the prayer warrior she is, she committed herself to my bedside and when she was not praying for me she was willing life into my body. I come from a family of prayer warriors and spiritual believers and they walk in the power of God.

The doctor told my family it was up to me to get better, let the truth be known, it had nothing to do with me, but all to do with God. When I got out of ICU, I had to learn how to walk which is very difficult and challenging however, during this time my brother and

I got closer. I realize how much he means to me and even if we don't see eye to eye on many things, he got my back and I got his. That was three years ago and I have made it through so much with the help of God and my family.

I used to take my family for granted; now I know they will be there when I need them and even if I do not think I need them. I told my daughter two months ago that I was positive and she told me she had an idea, so all this time I thought I had a secret but didn't. I felt relieved that she already knew which was a weight lifted off my shoulders. I joined a support group with women who have life stories just like mine and even though we are different in many ways, we are the same. I respect and love these women. Now I am getting my life together and there is a lot of work that I need to do.

Sincerely,

Sasha
Willing myself to live.

VALERIE

So how do you accept the fact that your only sister the one you look up to, the one that always had your back has the virus that causes AIDS? In my head this is my sister, my bread and butter the one that no matter how tough or how bad I had become she had my back. I do not know how you would deal with it, but the way I dealt with it was by getting high for a long time. I was in more denial then she was by telling myself the doctors made a mistake or maybe it is a bad dream, but this is the only dream that I was not going to wake up from.

I realized the true stigma that goes with the HIV virus. I was so worried that my sister was not going to be able to deal with being HIV positive, and although some people think she is a tough, strong hardcore person, she is not. She is a soft, fragile, gentle and caring person and she will cry in a drop of hat, believe me I know and I've seen her in action.

I believe the hardest part of my sister having the virus is the fact that I know so many people die from it. I don't want to deal with the fact that one day she won't be here when I need her. Now that I'm clean, sober and saved, I sit back and watch her every move. She amazes me, not once did she make her sickness about her so I decided that I would not make it about me losing her.

Every day I know it is a struggle for her but it doesn't show and you can tell by the work she is doing in her life to help other people come to grips with their status and by the way she reaches out to people with HIV and AIDS. I realize that I was the one who had an illness. My illness was not trusting God for the gift he gave my sister, the gift of being strong and having the will to complete the task that is put before her. My sister is Vanessa C. I love her. I am somebody in the name of Jesus Christ. That is the saying that our Pop–Pop Montgomery would say to us every day of our life and that saying caused the whole neighborhood to believe it. So, to my sister(s) remember I am somebody in the name of Jesus Christ.

Sincerely,

Valerie
My sister is strong.

SHARON

It was a cold winter night and I felt the midnight wind as it entered into my bedroom window. The street light gave my room a nightlight that made me feel comfortable and safe. My uncle came creeping in my bedroom like a snake. Not like any snake but the snake from The Garden of Eden. The one that spits lies like truth. It made Eve doubt what God said about the fruit. My uncle said he would not hurt me and that he loves me. However, his action was not what his words said. I have been haunted by his actions, which was a total violation of my humanity. My uncle was HIV positive and he knew it for years and here at the age of thirteen I was being infected.

Once I found out I was positive, I started using drugs just to be able to deal with all the crazy emotions that go with (as some people would say) a death sentence. Prostitution came along with it and before long I found myself in an apartment living with two men. I was their sexual partner and they would invite their friends over so I would exchange sex for money and drugs. I was talked about, misused, mistreated, mishandled and abused. You name it, and I have been through it.

Then one day I could not see the sunshine or the rain and I could no longer stand myself. God allowed a woman to come into my life and this woman of God told me things that no one should have known but God himself. She told me about my dreams and my secrets, and when she was done with me, I cried out to God and gave him my heart and my life and God accepted me as his own.

With the help from the sisters of the church, I now have my very own room. God took the taste of drugs from my mouth. I am in treatment for my HIV and doing very well I have a job and am going to school but most of all I have a relationship with God. I am no longer feeling sorry for myself. God has given me a life better than I could ever think. I have no problem telling my story because I know that I am not the only one out there in need of help.

Sincerely,

Sharon

I had fainted, unless I believed to see the goodness of the Lord in the land of the living. (Psalm 27: 13 King James)

JENNIFER

I don't have the virus my mother does. I really didn't think she had the virus because she is always laughing, and joking. I've never seen her depressed or real sick until a few years ago. I guess you can say I was in denial. I never heard my mom complain or say why me? My mom has always told me to protect myself.

In our house instead of having a candy dish, we had a condom dish. My friends would come to my house and snatch up condoms and sometimes my mom would have talks with them on how to protect themselves. It would drive me crazy but I would just brush it off and say that's just how she is, the self-made spokesperson of HIV and AIDS Educator. My mother would go out to school and speak about HIV and safe sex.

One day she came home and said, "baby girl (that's what she calls me when she got something to tell me and she don't think I'm going to take it well) how would you feel if I went to your school to tell them about the virus and let them know that I'm living with the virus." I told her, "Oh no you're not going to my school, and tell them nothing about you or the virus" she just looked at me and said "calm down I was just asking." Well, I wasn't ready for my mom to come to my school and talk about the virus or disclose that she has it. After all teenagers or should I say children can be very hateful and I would not be able to take people talking about my mother making silly remarks and just being plain rude.

Years have passed since that time, so I am blessed to see my mother speak about the virus at Worlds AIDS Day and I am so proud of her.

I know she is my mother and I am delighted to see a woman who is confident, sincere, daring, brave and even funny. I was in awe; my mom became my super hero that day. My mother has a lot of strength and I've seen her become a caregiver to my grandparents and that takes a lot of hard work and patience. I love my mom I thank God for her and she always says I will not die but live and proclaim the works of the Lord. (Psalm 118:17 King James) My mom is Vanessa C and she is my hero.

Sincerely,

Jennifer C
Love you forever.

ALLISON

In March 2006, I was in the hospital for MRSA. The doctor tested me for the virus that causes AIDS which came back negative. A few years later on December 4, 2008, I was hospitalized again for MRSA and again I took another test for the virus that causes AIDS and to my surprise, I was diagnosed with having the virus that causes AIDS. I was confused, upset and just plain crazy so I went to my boyfriend because I felt he needed to know. My heart was beating out of my chest wondering how I would tell him I was positive. I knew I had to tell him and the longer I would wait, the harder it would be for me to tell him. I know I will just have to say it straight and to the point. When I finally told him, there was no response. He wasn't upset, mad, angry or even confused, it was just like I told him that I put my favorite expensive panty hose on and my finger went through it. I would have gotten a better response from a stranger. Since I did not receive a response from him that left me feeling bitter, mad, confused, and I don't even know if I could put in words the emotions that I felt but yet it was a loneliness that is so unbelievable you just shake your head and pray that God has your back and that is just what I did.

One day I was at his apartment, so I decided to do some investigating. I looked through his medicine cabinet, his dresser drawers, between his sheets, mattress, and under the carpet. I found HIV medication, so I wrote down the names of the all the medications went to the internet, and found out what the medications were for. Let me make this clear so that people won't get the wrong idea because there are some medications that can be used for different illnesses, however HIV medication is only made for HIV illness therefore; I rest my case.

When I told him about my findings he denied it saying that medicine is not for HIV, it is for something else but he never said what it was for I guess he could not think of a lie quick enough.

I was shocked because the man that I gave my love, my heart and body to refused to tell me the truth even when I confronted him with everything and to top things off, we even went to the same doctor. I joined a wellness group and met women who are incredible and whenever I tell my story, they feel my pain. The members of the wellness group have said that he is not there yet and it takes time. So in my head I'm wondering how long will it take, then one woman said it took her years. What it all comes down to is I cannot make him be responsible for his actions, he is going to have to do it on his own. I'm only responsible for my actions and can only control my thinking and the things that I do. I will continue to pray for him, and will always remember that I am not alone because I have many sisters and we support each other.

Sincerely,

Allison
I am a responsible woman.

LAURA

In 1995, I took my daughter to her doctor's appointment. The doctor asked if he could give my daughter a test for HIV. When I asked why he said he did not like what he felt under her lymph nodes so I said sure. The doctor called me and told me to come in to get her result, which is when he told me that my daughter was HIV positive. I was in shock, confused, angry and I blamed myself because I was using drugs heavily. I continued to use, however, God gave me the right mindset to get my daughter into treatment.

I was tested in 1996, three days before my son was born, so I started taking AZT so that my son would have a chance to be safe. The Division of Youth and Family Services was going to take my children and separate them from me, so I had to get my life in order. I thank God for my family and friends that took my children in so that I could go into rehab. I met many wonderful women. When I got out of rehab I took my daughter to her doctor's appointment, I met a wonderful nurse who got me into a Ryan White program. She gave it to me straight and in a loving manner, so I will always have a tender spot in my heart for her. I became an advocate for HIV and joined various support groups. That nurse had a big impact in my life. I started going to church because without God I would not know where I would be.

I started working after seventeen years of being unemployed. I became a case manager and now I am doing testing and counseling. I thank God every day of my life for not allowing me to give up and for keeping me clean and sober for eight years. I have many great friends and family members care and trust me.

I joined a church that accepts me as I am and they know about my HIV status. I am the manager of a H.I.V. Ministry, which is an organization in my church for people infected and affected with the virus that causes AIDS. God is good to me! Never in a million years would I have thought my life would be this fulfilling. I thank God every day for letting me be who I am.

Sincerely,

Laura
For the kingdom of God is not in word, but in power (1Cor. 4:20 King James)

VANESSA

I remember just like it was yesterday. I was so excited as I went to my doctor's appointment because it was my first check up since I found out I was pregnant. So I was excited, happy and floating on air, after all this was the baby I asked God for. I was ready, but not for the information that my doctor would give me. I sat down in her office then she came in the office with what I call a straight forward move. The words that came out of her mouth were; your blood work shows that you are HIV positive and I can no longer treat you here, so you'll have to go to a high-risk clinic, goodbye. I felt a chill take over my body and somehow I totally went into left field instead of running to first base, I ran to third base and it seems like I have been running ever since.

Four months after my diagnosis, my aunt and mother went to the hospital to see a family member. A woman was crying hysterically so my aunt asked her what was wrong and she stated her brother just died from AIDS. With that information my aunt came to tell me and when I heard the name again, I ran in left field because he was an old boyfriend. I can remember the first time I met him. I knew all the girls wanted him and because of the things my auntie taught me about men it was those things that allowed me to be the one that would get him. When we would have sex he always went into the bathroom and would come out with a towel wrapped around his arms with drops of blood on the towel. Although I didn't understand it then, now when I look back, I remembered that he used to be a drug user and he used to shoot heroin and that's when my world shattered. My mother and I went to the wake, and she wanted to destroy him, break his glasses, snatch his tie off, take his suit off and put him face down in the casket. So it took everything inside me to make my mother not follow through with that assignment. I told her if he knew his status, then he wouldn't have given it to me. At least that's what I wanted to believe.

My baby is healthy and does not show any sign of the virus that causes AIDS. Thank God! I went into a deep denial and my actions were hurtful, harmful and selfish. Many years had passed and God allowed me to get sick. Sick enough to know that I had to look up and recognize God and realize that I am only here because God has a plan for my life. I could never go back and take away the pain that I caused people. However, I can speak out and let people know that I am here and having HIV is not what I am it is what I have. It does not stop me from serving God or speaking out. Present your body as a living sacrifice holy and acceptable unto God, which is your reasonable act of worship. (Romans 12:1 King James)

Sincerely,

Vanessa
I shall not die but live and proclaim the works of the Lord. (Psalm 118:17 King James)

LEAH

I found out I was positive when a good friend of mind found out she was positive and convinced me to be tested. That was two years ago and I still feel numb. I do not know who gave it to me and to be honest I just don't care. I have a disease that is going to make me sick, take my dignity and allow people to look at me as if I did something so perverted to get this disease which I did not. I just had intercourse with someone who had the AIDS virus.

I am scared all of the time. I am twenty-one years old and I want to have a husband and give birth to my own child. I just cannot see myself having a baby and not knowing if the baby is going to have this virus. I have gone to a few women's groups and I have heard what they were saying but these women are older and have their children and husband. I have to say this, I do not want to sound mean but these women have lived their lives. Although I am still young, I've stopped going to parties because I don't want to get drunk and find myself in bed with a man and not have any protection. I've stopped being young minded. My best friend passed away last year and she was the only one I could talk to. We would laugh for hours and she would always tell me that we can have a life; we just have to be comfortable in our own skin and trust God.

I am only telling my story now because of a young woman who was doing my hair told me about her aunt that has the virus and is writing a book about women with the HIV virus. So since they did not have to use their name and she let me read her aunts' story I decided to share. That was the first time I ever felt like I needed to tell my story, and that I needed to get involved and become alive. It's time to start letting young girls know that you have to protect yourself no matter what because it can happen to you like it happened to me.

Sincerely,

Leah
Living life with no excuses.

ROBIN

I was dating my first love and he was so beautiful to me. His skin was creamy peanut butter brown and his hair was dirty brown. He had dimples that you could put cherries in and his smile was wide with teeth that were white as snow. He also enjoyed all types of people. When I started hearing rumors that he was gay, I just figured people didn't like him because he talked to any and everybody so I just stopped listening to the gossip. I found out I was pregnant and they tested me for HIV and it came back positive. I told the nurse that I needed a do over so that I could pass the test and maybe it was something in the lab so she tested me again and it came back positive again. I went directly to my mother's house (who is a Christian) and told her that I was positive and I wanted to have an abortion. I knew my mom would not have agreed to that but I had to throw it out there. She told me God has a plan for my life and that she gave me to God while I was still in her wound and that was the promise that she had made to God. I could do many things but fighting God was not one of them.

I listened to her advice and she wanted me to go tell the father of the baby and to come right back and I did just that. So I told him that I was HIV positive and pregnant and he then began accusing me of cheating on him and I was devastated. I do not know what bothered me the most, being HIV positive or him saying I cheated on him. I couldn't even argue with him because I just kept hearing my mother voice saying God has a plan for you so go get you things and come back home and that is just what I did, I got my things and left. When

Vanessa G. Cheek

I was four months pregnant I saw my ex-boyfriend all hugged up with some old man, then I knew it was not a rumor, he was a homosexual.

I thought I was going to lose my mind. I wanted an abortion, but when I spoke to a nurse she told me just because I had the virus does not mean my child will have it and if I take the medication like I'm supposed to and get my baby on medication for a year then the baby should be fine. It has been five years and my daughter is doing well without any trace of the virus.

My mother was right, my affliction was only for a moment and it taught me how to trust in God for many things. I am born again and it feels good. I love the Lord with all my heart and I will try not to lean on my own understanding.

Sincerely,

Robin
Affliction will not last forever.

RITA

While I was in prison in 1993, I was tested for the virus that causes AIDS, which came back positive. I did not believe it because it was the prison system performing the test and since so many prisoners were being tested that there was no way my test was accurate, so I just acted as if I never had taken the test. In my mind, I knew the test had to be true but when you're locked up there is so much stress that denial is the best way to deal with the problems you can't face.

When I got out of prison I went to a clinic to be tested, again it came back positive. I told my sisters because I had to tell someone but when I got alone I went to God and asked him why me? Why are you doing this to me? I grew up with you in my life God and this is how you are going to treat me. For a brief moment God allowed me to have clarity and then the words I heard was stop you left me and although I gave you free will, the lifestyle you have chosen was not the life I had for you. I just started to cry because it was all true.

Later I met a man who had a two-bed room apartment and he wanted to rent out one of the bedrooms. I asked to rent it and he agreed. I didn't think I had to tell him about my status because I knew we were not going to be intimate, but six months later we were in a relationship. I did not know how to tell him but I knew I had to but I did not want to be rejected. I came out and told him and surprisingly he took it very well, he just wanted to know everything about HIV and AIDS. We got married and had a child together and although I would love to say I live an ideal life and everything is perfect but it's not. I have older children and my past actions have caused so much pain for them that they believe I don't love them because of the lifestyle that I lived. I cannot make it up to them so I just pray that one day they can find it in their hearts to forgive me.

Sincerely,

Rita
Communicate with your children.

ANGIE

When I was pregnant with my second child seven years ago, I found out I was positive with the virus that causes AIDS. All I could think about was how I would tell me boyfriend. He was not my baby's father so if he did the math, he would realize it too.

My baby's father is a married man who has the virus. We had the type of relationship that when I needed money I would go to him sexually whenever I needed a bill paid, new clothes or whatever else I needed. I thought it was worth the risk and I have made many bad decisions especially for not telling him (my boyfriend) that I was positive. I just could not reveal my HIV status because when I told him I was pregnant his eyes lit up and he had such a big beautiful smile that I just could not tell him.

Three years after our child was born (who is negative thank God for the medication they gave him and me)I told my boyfriend that we should go and get tested for HIV and AIDS. I also told him that I wanted us to be around for our son, so he agreed. We went for our HIV test. His test result came back negative, and I was surprised, puzzled and pleased so I tried not to show it. So when my test result came back positive, he looked up at my face and broke down saying oh baby I am so sorry and he said it over and over again. I could not help but cry uncontrollable not because I have the virus but because he loves me so much.

I wanted to come clean and tell him everything, but when I looked into his face, I just could not hurt him anymore. We are still together and we're engaged. I wanted people to know that there is love after you get HIV positive results, everyone needs love, and there is love out there for everyone.

Sincerely,

Angie
I got love!

TYRONE

I am the oldest of three children and my mother was a hopeless drug addict. At the age of twelve, I had to take care of my brother and sister and to some extent my mother too. I always knew that I was different than the rest of the boys in my school because when they were interested in girls I was interested in boys. I had no interest in girls unless they wanted me to do their hair, dress them for prom or when they were going out on a date.

At fifteen, I just knew I was in love when I met a boy who was very interested in me. So what if he had a girlfriend, he was the first boy who showed an interest in me. He wanted me sexually so we did it and after it happened, I never bragged about it. I am not one that would kiss and tell. After dealing with him for a couple of years, I just didn't want to be bothered with him anymore so I called it off. Being a gay teenager is extremely difficult and compounded with not knowing how to deal with it, well I began to drink, drug, sex it up and party. In 1993 while I was locked up was when I found out I was HIV positive and due to the fact that I wasn't an IV drug user I knew it had to be my homosexual lifestyle. Someone asked, how I got the virus, but I really cannot say who gave it to me because I do not know.

In 2002, I met a woman who was HIV positive and she dealt with having the virus differently than anyone else I knew. She stated since I got it, I'm going to deal with it and there's no need to cry about it. Instead, let's talk about it, laugh about it and live with it. I felt the same way, and because of her I started going to support groups.

The first person I told my status to was my grandmother; she was calm, comforting and showed me love. Having the virus made me more aware of life. I do not take too many things for granted. I have a support team for the times when I am going through something that is too hard for me to deal with it on my own. I can call my friend, who laughs and jokes about having HIV and that always makes me feel better. There are people that we hang with that do not understand laughing about the virus and they get mad at us. People need to know laughter heals the soul if you cannot laugh at yourself who can you laugh at.

Sincerely,

Tyrone
Laugh and love yourself.

HATTIE

As long as I could remember, I never liked to be alone; I guess being the only child had something to do with it. My mother worked constantly and my father lived across town with his family, so I never had a chance to spend any time with him. I would see him occasionally when we bumped into each other at the same store, or when he drove passed us. The older I got the lonelier I felt so I made up my mind that I would never be alone.

When the first boy began acting as if he liked me, I gave myself to him. I just knew it was love at first sight, but after a few days he stopped coming by and the next boy would come along so I would give myself to him and would get the same result. When I got to junior high, I was called a whore that was never good enough to date but good enough to have sex with, and with all the names that I was called really left me depressed. I tried to commit suicide many times and failed. My mother finally got tired of me, so she sent me away to my aunt who lived down south.

I met a young man and knew it was love at first sight so we got married. I already knew he was a cheater, so he began to bring women home and we had threesome for years, because I would do anything to please him. One day I got sick and went to the doctor's office but they could not figure out what was wrong with me, until they did many blood tests and the one special test told me all I needed to know, I was HIV positive. When I told my husband, he looked at me, laughed and said okay what you want me to do. I couldn't believe it, so at first I just stood there and cried but when I got myself together I started packing and I didn't know where I was going but I was getting out there. I went to my aunt's house and I told her everything. She told me to make a six month plan, so I did it and within six months, I had job, filed for a divorce and got myself an apartment. I also made flyers with my husbands' picture on it and the caption in big bold red letters that said please do not sleep with me I have AIDS. I put them up around in the clubs, grocery stores and just about everywhere I went, I put up a flyer and that made me feel much better.

People, there is no such thing as love at first sight, but there is lust and physical attraction but real love only comes when you get to know someone and they get to know you. I'm not lonely anymore because I found Jesus, well actually he found me.

Sincerely,

Hattie
Never alone.

CARL

I remember my sister as if it was yesterday, with her skin tone like milk chocolate that was very smooth and she had a cleft in her chin and we used to tease her about it. She always wanted to help people so one day she brought one of her classmates home, and gave her a bath and clean clothes. She begged our mother to do the poor little girl's hair and my mother was so mad at her but she did the girl's hair any way and gave her clothes that my sister couldn't fit. That is just how my sister has been, always wanting to help even if people did not want help.

When my sister was diagnosed, I think I took it harder than she did. I immediately went looking for her boyfriend and God knows if I would have found him, I could have got myself into a big mess. My sister still loved this man and I was looking at her as if she was out of her mind. So I asked her why was she still with this guy. She simply looked at me and said because I love him. As she looked at me, she shook her head then rolled her eyes and said don't worry about me I'm going to be alright. How could I not worry about her? She is my baby sister the only sister I've had all of my life that I've worried about and now she wants to release me from my job.

My sister suddenly moved out of the state, and I believed she moved because she didn't want me to worry about her or help her in anyway. Once, she had told me that I was a control freak and that I thought I could make everything better when I didn't have the power. Then I had the nerve to start crying and she started laughing at me. While she was away, she got sick and I couldn't be by her side so I was a wreck until she finally got well enough to come back to New Jersey. I tried to spend every day with her. I remember sitting by her bedside at the hospital, and I told her that if I could take her place I would because I wanted her to live forever and she looked at me and said no oh no I don't want to be in your shoes because you are going to have to deal with mommy.

On December 25, I went to see my sister early in the morning because I wanted to be first to wish her a Merry Christmas and as I stepped in her room and gave her a kiss to wish her a Merry Christmas, she said I'm ready to go home. I told her that if she really wanted to go then it's going to be okay. One hour later, she was gone. My sister died on December 25th at 2:00 p.m. and I was there holding her hands. Just like on our first day at Sunday school. It's so funny the things you can remember when your mind is in another state.

Sincerely,

Carl
My sister's keeper

SANDY

I was born into this world by two heavy drug addicted parents so one might say that because I watched my parents get high and I've seen their downfall, then I should have learned from their mistakes. I would love to say that I had learned from them but that would be a lie. The way my parents lived their lives was always very exciting to me. My dad would get locked up, and while he was in prison my mother and I would go visit him. My mom made me carry the drugs in my hair ribbons or she would even insert the drugs inside me then I would ease it out after the guard would turn his back. When my mother got tired of seeing my dad locked up she started going out with a drug dealer and that was a real good thing because we would shop until we dropped and the money was really flowing.

Whenever I wanted extra money, my mother's boyfriend would give me a package to sell and that was all I needed. I was selling and using until it got to the point that I was using more than I was selling and then I started the unenviable; I started stealing drugs. So once my mom broke up with her boyfriend, I had to do other things to support my habit and that's when I got into prostitution. When I heard a trick I had was HIV positive I just figured I must be positive too. Therefore I lived my life as if I was positive. I became clean in 2005 and I decided to be tested so I was shocked when the test came back HIV negative. I immediately requested that they do the test over. There had to be a mistake because I have always had risky behaviors and the people I chose to get high with and share the same needle with were people who I knew were either HIV positive or they had AIDS. So this negative test result had to be a mistake but it wasn't a mistake, I did not have the virus that can cause AIDS at least not at that time.

I was tested again in September 2006 and that's when my results came back HIV positive but I am not mad at myself, or anyone else because of the way I lived. I always thought if anyone should have the virus why not me. Actually if the truth be told, my dad died in prison from AIDS. My mother died from the virus one year ago so I believe I am living my destiny.

I believe now my life has taken on a different journey because now I believe I must speak up about HIV and AIDS and bring it to the forefront so that no one else becomes infected with this disease.

Sincerely,

Sandy
My destiny

WILLIAM

I am familiar with HIV and AIDS. I know a few people who live with it and died from it. My belief about HIV and AIDS are very different from other people and the reason that I'm not scared of it is because I read about it so it does not bother me at all. I believe that everyone has the virus that causes AIDS, it is just not active. That is only my belief.

I'm dating a woman that has the virus and when I look at her I don't see the virus. I guess what I'm saying is that the virus does not define her. She is very careful about the things she says and does with me and it drives me crazy because sometimes I just want to say live and stop being so careful.

One night we were making love and it was very passionate but when the condom broke she flipped out and I had to tell her to relax because if I'm going to get it there is nothing you can do. Being extra careful is just not going to prevent it from happening. There have been times when we were making love and our love is so powerful that I feel like becoming infected is worth the risk. I know how crazy that may sound to some of you but I'm very much in love with this woman. To tell you the truth I have been in love with her since the seventh grade. We have much history together and she knows me like no other.

She has accused me of wanting the virus. Sometimes I believe I do, you see I lost my mother a few years ago and I miss her like crazy. I never had the chance to say good-bye or tell her that I was sorry for the way I lived or the way I treated her. That is the most difficult thing I have had to deal with. I guess what I am saying is people act like

HIV and AIDS is the worst thing that can happen to you but I look at addiction or dealing with the loss of loved ones, rape victims and child abuse, all these things can be devastating. Therefore, it's hard to say what is worst because you cannot put any of these in a category. I believe because of dealing with this woman has also made me ready to deal with some of my emotional baggage.

I realize for some people contracting HIV or AIDS maybe a death sentence but for some people it is a rebirth, which means they've started living their lives instead of just existing. If I ever get this virus, not that I am expecting to get HIV but if I do, I want to be one of the ones who starts living.

Sincerely,

William

Loving my lady.

TRACEY

It was a hot sunny day in the neighborhood and everyone was outside. The children were playing and the nosey neighbors outside gossiping. Out of nowhere my cousin and I began to argue but I couldn't even tell you what the argument was about the only thing that I can recall is seeing my cousin standing in the middle of the street and in front of everyone she screamed out, THAT'S WHY YOU GOT AIDS. I was devastated and heartbroken and everything appeared to be moving in slow motion.

The children that were playing in the middle of the street had come to a complete stop and they began to stare at me. My nosey neighbors now had more stuff to talk about and although I tried to run and get out of the way of the piercing eyes, they had still followed me. I did not see this coming and as I stood there in total silence my cousin told my whole life story with just those few words, you got AIDS. I thought I was running but I later realize that I had actually collapsed in the middle of the street.

When I regained consciousness, my neighbor Mrs. J was standing over me and then she helped me up. Mrs. J immediately brought me inside her house and then she sent her grandchildren out. She told me to never ever feel alone because you're not and don't worry about what people might say or think about you as long as you're alive and you can take care of yourself there is always hope. If you need me, I am here and whatever you tell me will never be heard out in the streets. After she said those words something happened to me as my burdensome how seemed lighter and I finally felt like I could breathe.

The secret that I had kept for four years had taken such a toll on me that I didn't realize how much stress I was under and thank God for Mrs. J. We were good friends so I could tell her things and I haven't heard anything that I said in the streets. Why Mrs. J came to my rescue and befriended me, well I may never know but I am glad she did. Now I live without secrets and as for my cousin, well I didn't want to forgive her but I did. The stress of not forgiving her would destroy my immune system and I really want to live today without secrets.

Sincerely

Tracey
No secrets

NICOLE

I'm one hundred and twenty-five pounds, five feet three inches tall, with long black shiny hair. I keep my eyebrows waxed, and my make-up is always perfect. I have an apple bottom booty and tiny waist, which is only one reason why I am known as that chick. I moved to New York because I was told I could make much money being a dancer and let's face it, since I have the body, the looks and enjoy dancing that made my decision easy so that's just what I did.

Although I was making good money, I started living beyond my means and that is when my demise started. One of the girls told me that I could make extra money by doing after party dates. An after party date occurs when you're dancing for a guy and he is willing to spend extra money on you after the club closes but the bottom line is you're exchanging sexual favors for cash. Actually let's keep it real, it is prostitution and I was okay with what I was doing.

Just to be able to deal with the drama that I was going through emotionally, physically, mentally and spiritually I started using cocaine. After three years of doing the sex exchange for money I found out one of the exchange girls (that is what we call each other) was diagnosed with the virus that cause AIDS. With that information, all of the girls decided it was time for us to be tested and out of seven of us, five were diagnosed and I was one out of five.

When I told my sister I had the virus, she told me it was because of my homosexual tendencies and taking hormone shots to have breast and with all of the other girly things I've done I should be blessed that was all that was wrong with me. I was devastated and told her my sexuality had nothing to do with me getting the virus it was my behavior. If you do not know it by now, I am finally being liberated from a man body.

People must stop being so judgmental because AIDS is not just for homosexuals, it is not prejudice, so be ever so careful. You never know if you will be next.

Sincerely

Nicole
It's not a gay thing.

BRENDA

It was Thanksgiving Day and I was at my aunt's house, which became our family ritual. This was a good thing because when my grandmother died five years ago it stopped a lot of family members from getting together but this Thanksgiving was very different than any other. Well after many years of living my life with no boundaries I found out I contracted HIV and I wanted to be with my family. In my mind this was going to be my last family gathering because it wasn't HIV that was going to take me out it was going to be the embarrassment that was going to allow me to end my life. I had made up my mind and in my pocketbook were the pills needed to complete my task.

My brother brought his girlfriend to our Thanksgiving dinner. She was different from the other women he had dated and she was a delight to be around. She had a strength about her as if she could handle anything, and that must be true since she has been dating my brother for six months. My brother seems to have changed and it was nice to hear him talking about God. He even prayed over dinner and that was something to give thanks too.

I had to get to know this woman who changed my brother. Don't ask me why, I just needed to talk to her so when I went out for a cigarette I asked her to join me she gave my brother a look and then she said, "Here goes." We went outside and she said, "I know you must have concerns about me being HIV positive. Your brother and some of your family members know and I wanted to be the one to tell you but before she could say another word I just stopped her and asked, "how do you do it, I'm ready to end my life and you are so strong and secure how could you be that strong?" She just looked at me and asked, "How long have you known that you were positive?" Before I knew it, I had told my whole life story and between the tears and laughter I realized that I've found a new friend.

We talked about everything including our medications, and support groups. She even went to my doctor's appointments. We go to church on Sunday and bible study on Wednesday. Now I know how she does it. She attends a support group and she has support from her church and God, and she prays a lot. My brother proposed to her and they are getting married and I finally have an older sister. I don't call her my sister-in-law because I prefer to call her my sister-in-love, and she has loved me from the minute I met her. As for the pills I once had in my pocketbook to end my life well she took them and told me that I will never need them again. What a true statement that was.

Sincerely,

Brenda
Thanksgiving

DINA

In December 2000, it was freezing outside and as much as I wanted to stay in bed, I went to my doctor's appointment because I thought I had food poisoning and that's when found out I was pregnant and HIV positive. What a shocking surprise it was to receive such news which is why I had a lot of mixed emotions and the only thing that came to my mind was wow God must really think I am special so with that thought process, I decided to blame God. It couldn't possibly be my behavior that caused me to be HIV positive.

I was determined not to tell anyone. I had a nurse that made it her business to be an HIV advocate so every time I wanted to blame God or any other people she would say, "So you had no other choice, you couldn't say put on this condom." After hearing that for eight months it made me rethink my actions. Now when I say God must have thought I was special I realize that it's true and mean it without being sarcastic. Having HIV didn't destroy me instead it gave me strength that I didn't know I had. Do not get me wrong it took me a long time to get where I am today.

I went into denial that left me devastated, confused, mad and even crazy. I started drinking and doing drugs because I was hurt and the only way I could deal with it was by numbing myself. Did it work? No. What really helped me was the nurse that God sent my way to tell me that drinking and doing drugs was not the way to go if I wanted to have a healthy baby. With that information, I decided to do the correct thing. I could go on and on but the bottom line is God is still on the throne and I am so proud of my son. He is a joy and in his own right, he is an academy award winner. My son is HIV negative and I'm so excited.

Sincerely,

Dina
God must think I am special, I am.

DARWIN

I'm a professional trainer, so I understand the human body and I know what it takes mentally and physically to get your body in shape. I love the way the body takes form when you exercise and eat the proper food. I opened my own gym and was ready to take my career to another level. I was even ready to settle down with my girl who I was dating for seven years and it was about time. My girl had been nagging me for over two years, so today would be the day that I propose to her.

My girlfriend called to tell me that we needed to talk face to face. So I thought I would have to hear her say how she's spent too much of her time to be just my girl and that she needs more and if we're not going to get married then she's out of here. Imagine how surprised I was when the talk I was expecting turned out to be something totally different. The talk was simple with her stating that she had been tested for having the virus that causes AIDS and that her result was positive.

I was in shock and disbelief. I thought I was standing on my feet until I felt my legs give out from underneath me. My girl told me to get tested and offered to go with me. So we went and my result was HIV positive. I've never did any drugs, never cheated on any of my girlfriends and I've never had any homosexual relationships. To be honest I don't know how I got the virus that causes AIDS. I'm just glad that my woman got tested and told me her result so we have been able to be very open and honest with each other. The talk that I was waiting for her to have with me, well it turned the other way around because I had to have the talk with her. We consulted with our doctors about our condition and both doctors gave us their blessings.

On August 4, 2007 the love of my life and I tied the knot. We are very happy. My business is booming, our health is great and we are enjoying life on life terms.

Sincerely,

Darwin
Life on life terms.

MARIE

I would really want people to think that once I found out I was HIV positive, then I started doing the correct thing but that would be a lie. I could tell you a lie and some of you would most likely believe it because everyone would like to believe in or read a happily ever after but every story does not end with happily ever after, so here's my story.

I actually found out I was positive May 5, 1997, which is when I gave birth to my son Louis. He was beautiful with jet-black curly hair, smooth hot chocolate skin and he weighed 6 lbs. 3 ounces and was 18 inches long. When I looked at him, I knew he was an angel. I wasn't supposed to breast feed because of my diagnosis, so I was total pissed off because I come from a family that believes all women must breastfeed and I was not going up against that tradition. So, since I was told not to breastfeed then that meant I had to be honest by telling my parents that I am HIV positive or live in denial and breastfeed. So as soon as I took my baby home, I started breastfeeding.

Three months after I brought my baby home he became sick and was hospitalized then six months later, my son died because of complications from AIDS. I kept that secret until now and I blame myself for my baby's death. I hate the fact that I was too embarrassed to let any of my family members know that I am infected. Even now, there are times that I have to keep my secret. When I meet a man in a club, we laugh, talk, drink, then when it's time to have sex I tell them to use condoms. So, if they don't then it's not my fault because everyone should know that there is HIV and AIDS out there as well as other sexually transmitted diseases. I am not going to be the only responsible person just because I know I have AIDS. People should know that not everyone is truthful and they should be responsible for their own action.

Being responsible is not just for the people who have HIV or AIDS. If you are sexually active, you should be responsible. So although I'm not going around telling everyone that I have HIV because that is my personal business but I will always tell you to use a condom however, if you feel like playing Russian roulette it is on you. I am not a carrier of a gun, but I am a carrier of condoms.

Sincerely,

Marie
I will not take the blame because you think everyone should be honest.

LOVELY

On July 2005, my grandmother sat me down to have a long tearful complicated talk. At first, I thought it was going to be the sex talk but it would not be that easy. My grandmother had decided to tell me at thirteen years old that I was born with HIV. Although the words sounded very strange coming out of her mouth, I must have looked very strange to her because she kept asking are you all right are you all right. That's when I knew I had taken a trip from my body because I could no longer see my nana; I just heard her voice. Finally, what felt like a few seconds, was actually a couple of hours.

As I sat on the back porch, I believed that I knew something was wrong with me because I was always taking medication. I never thought I was infected. I thought I knew how my mother had died, because my family would always say she had cancer. I wanted answers because I wondered why they didn't say anything when I was young. It couldn't be that they thought I would tell people besides who was I going to tell my grandmother who raised me and kept me so close to her skirt to make sure that I had no friends.

I spoke to my aunt and she explained that my mom had the virus, which is how I became prenatally infected. Although my father wanted her to abort me, my mom was not going to do that because she always wanted to be a mother and have a daughter. It didn't take long for my father to leave so my mother had to raise me. She named me Lovely because when she looked at me she just wanted to love me up and that's what she did until the day she died. I wanted to be mad, but I couldn't because my mom left handwritten love letters and videos of her loving me up. Even though I have the virus, I'm okay because I know how much my mom loved me. My mom even gave me instructions on how to deal with my status.

I'm Lovely
That's my name

New Jersey AIDS Hotline
In New Jersey (800) 624—2377
If calling out of State (609) 984—5874
TTY/TDD (201) 926-8008
24 hours 7 days a week

Website Information: www.hab.hrsa.gov

The above website contains HIV prevention messages that may not be appropriate for all audiences. Since HIV infections are spread primarily through sexual practices and sharing needles, the prevention message and program may address these topics. If you are not seeking such information or may be offended, please do not go to the website.